# Child Genius 101

The Ultimate Early Childhood Development Program

# Child Genius 101

## The Ultimate Early Childhood Development Program

by Phillip J. Chipping
with Savannah Hendricks

Phillip J. Chipping | Savannah Hendricks
Child Genius 101 - The Ultimate Early Childhood Development Program

Summary: eductaion, early childhood development, self-help, educational resource book for parents of young children

ISBN: 978-0-9859378-4-3

Printed in the U.S.A.
First American Edition, October, 2013.

# Table of *Contents*

!*

Dedicated to all new parents in the world. We hope this book will help you as you embark on the toughest and best job in the whole world.

- Phillip & Savannah

# **Preface:** *by the authors*

You've read the title of the book and of course the first question on your mind is this:

"Is it really possible to help my baby become a genius?"

"Are there actual steps I can take now to help her be ready for school, to excel from kindergarten to college, and to grow up more prepared for the workplace and life in general?"

The answer?

**Yes.**

A definitive, absolute, research-backed and resounding ***YES!***

Research has proven that "there is **one prekindergarten skill** that matters above all others, because it is the **prime predictor** of school success or failure."1

The best part? It's not expensive at all. In fact, it turns out that the most effective thing you can do to prepare your child for school and life is also the least expensive!

It's all right here for under $10.00

This book does two things. First, it will give you insight into the groundbreaking research surrounding early childhood development. Second, it shows you how to implement that research in your own life and family, easily and effectively with fun activities and more, every single day.

We hope you enjoy the activities and adventures that await!

Phillip J. Chipping // Founder
*knowonder!* publishing
www.knowonder.com

Savannah Hendricks //
Staff Writer

# Why You Should Care

## The Research:

In 1996 a landmark research study was published in the field of Early Childhood Development.[1] The study was so groundbreaking in its findings and claims that it has spurred hundreds of ancillary research studies and thousands of citations.

In that study, Dr. Betty Hart and Dr. Todd R. Risley demonstrated a direct correlation between **one specific action which resulted in profound gains** in literacy, education success and IQ in children entering kindergarten.[2]

That one action had such a profound effect on the children in the study that the results lasted five years, ten years, fifteen years and more! Indeed, it has impacted their lives forever.

In other words, one specific action had the ability to increase a child's IQ in a way that affected them for the long term.

In addition to that, their research clearly showed the world that the most important and most formative years of a child's brain (and educational) development was between the ages of 0-3, long before that child would ever enter a preschool let alone a public school.

Their study also showed that despite the very best efforts by preschools and public education systems to bring the children with lower scoring IQs up-to-par with the children ranking in the middle and upper scores, it was virtually impossible for a school teacher to make up the difference for what had transpired in the home before that child ever came to school.

And to top it off, their research showed that when performed in the home, the same single action leveled the playing field for children later in school, irrespective of socio-economic status, income level, gender or race. It could literally break the cycle of poverty in just one generation!

In his book and treatise on the subject of innovation in education, Disrupting Class, Harvard professor and world-renowned leader on innovation Clayton Christensen says the following regarding this research study:

"A rather stunning body of research is emerging that suggests that starting these reforms at kindergarten, let alone in elementary, middle or high school, is far too late. By some estimates, 98 percent of education spending occurs after the basic intellectual capacities of children have mostly been determined...

This particular strand of research is teaching us that a significant portion of a person's intellectual capacity is determined in his or her first 36 months."[3]

He goes on to say that the most powerful time is during a person's first year of life - "when there [is] no visible evidence that the child [can] understand what the parents [are] saying."

And yet, despite all of the research that has been done on the topic, there has been virtually no implementation of the findings in a meaningful way. Governments are only set up to start spending on a child's education beginning at the age of five. There is only one other commercial product or service available to families to help implement the research findings, but it costs a whopping $700+ and is logistically challenging to implement, as well. (Don't misunderstand - it's a good product and it has great reviews and research behind it).

But the "secret" is so simple and costs so little that we felt we had to create this book series to help the regular and lower-income families. The ones who can't afford $700 upfront. The ones who really need and want the help.

Indeed, this one action is the most inexpensive thing a parent can give their children (outside of hugs and love).

# The Secret:

So what is the secret? The secret is simply this - proactively and intentionally talking and reading to your child. In essence, the more families speak and read to their babies, the smarter their babies will be.

In fact, the research showed a direct correlation between the size of a child's vocabulary upon entering kindergarten, their IQ, and how well they did in school for the rest of their lives. The size of their vocabulary (not words they could read or speak, but words they could understand) made all the difference.

Here is what national reading expert Jim Trelease says on the subject:

**"There is one prekindergarten skill that matters above all others because it is the**

***prime predictor* of school success or failure: the child's *vocabulary* upon entering school."**[4]

Makes sense, right?

Simple, right?

Yes and yes.

# So Why Do You Need This Book?

There are a two main reasons why this book is so valuable in helping achieve the results you desire with your child.

## Reason #1 - The Common Lexicon Problem

As parents, we often get into a daily routine (sometimes better known as a rut) and our vocabulary becomes as restricted and small as do our daily activities and personal experiences. In fact, most adults only use 5,000 to 10,000 words (called the "common lexicon") in their daily lives. But it is the "rare" words above and beyond those 10,000 that truly determine a child's literacy level.[5]

The daily topics in this book help you think and talk about something new and different each day so the vocabulary you use can be broadened without any effort or difficult daily planning on your part. Just open the book to the new day and you will have a new topic with lots of new vocabulary words to talk about.

The importance of this aspect cannot be overstressed. In order to grow your child's vocabulary, they must hear more words. The more words they hear, the higher their IQ, and the better-programmed their brain. This book is a virtual goldmine in vocabulary words and interaction opportunities! And when you use vocabulary words in a way that reinforces them with interaction, you are helping cement those words into your child's brain.

## Reason #2 - Small and Simple Things

Small and simple things, done over and over and over again, create truly powerful and profound results. It is a basic principle of life, as sound and true as the law of gravity.

Unfortunately, sometimes it's those easy things we know we need to do that are often left undone. Like working out each day. Or eating healthy food each day.

To talk proactively and intentionally to your child is difficult because it takes daily effort, especially to do it in a way that keeps the parent and child engaged day after day after day.

This book exists to help you actually DO the work to build your child's vocabulary. It provides you with well-prepared, daily tools. It helps remind you to do the work, each and every day. And it makes talking to your child easy, effective, and FUN!

## Why Is Talking So Important?

Here are just a few direct quotes from the research studies to illustrate why talking to your child each day is so important.

> "With few exceptions, the more parents talked to their children, the faster their children's vocabularies grew and the higher the children's IQ test scores were at ages three and up."[6]

> "The children whose parents did not begin speaking seriously to their children until their children could speak, at roughly age 12 months, suffered a persistent deficit in intellectual capacity, compared to those whose parents were talkative from the beginning."[7]

> "Conversation is the prime garden in which vocabularies grow."[8]

Think about it for a minute. Which child will be better prepared for school? Which one will best be able to understand the teacher's words? The one who has heard 46 million words spoken in his home before coming to school? Or the one who has only heard 13 million? That is the difference between the average "talkative" (high-income) family vs. the average "non-talkative" (poverty-level) family, according to the research quoted previously.[9]

(It's interesting to note that the most-talkative families are usually the most well-educated families. But it doesn't have to be that way! This program is designed to get ALL parents talking to their children the way doctors and lawyers do, and give all children the same pre-school advantages. Utilizing this resource every day can literally break the cycle of poverty in just one generation.)

Consider the HUGE gap between the two examples above - 13 million words vs. 46 million. We know a child's brain is capable of learning and understanding almost ALL of those words by the time they are five. Their capacity to learn language is amazing. For example, children in multi-cultural areas of the world are known to learn two, three, even four and five languages by the time they are five years old. So we know their brains have enormous potential to capture, figure out, and understand the meaning of new words. And they do it all simply by listening.

It makes sense, then, that the child who hears more words will be better prepared for school AND for life.

Every aspect of school has to do with literacy in one shape or another. There is a saying in the world of education: "Learn to read, then read to learn."

So, obviously, before a child ever begins reading, she must learn to read. How? By listening. A child must listen to a teacher. The first four years of public school are primarily oral education. But if the student does not understand some of the words the teacher is saying she will begin falling behind immediately.

After third grade, a child must be able to read independently in order to learn (read to learn). The teacher is still very involved, but much of the learning must now happen through text that is assigned to the child to read.

If a student was already falling behind during the listening phase of learning, she will only continue on a downward spiral as the teaching transitions into this new reading phase.

To make matters worse, in today's busy world more parents are working longer hours than ever before. It is critical for us to take proactive steps to ensure our children are hearing the words they need to hear inside our homes during the time we DO have available to spend with them. No amount of school can ever make up for what a child misses in the home.

Child Genius 101 is designed to help fill this need.

# How to Use This Book:

This book is broken down into daily segments. Each daily segment features five areas: Talk Time, Questions, Vocabulary Words, Activities, and Resources. Let's look at each one.

Talk Time: Each Talk Time segment gives you three or four "prompts" to help jog your memory and make it easier to talk about the topic at hand.

**Questions:** The question segment can be used two ways. First, if you have an infant, use the questions to help you think of even more things to say and explore regarding the topic. Second, if your child is old enough to respond, ask your child the questions. You may want to ask your child the questions even if he can't respond! We know that children understand what we're saying long before they can respond, so asking them questions is also a great way to get their brains thinking and working.

**Vocabulary:** Each daily topic comes complete with a big list of corresponding vocabulary words. Try to use as many of these words throughout the day as you explore the daily topic with your child. (Speaking of vocabulary, be sure to check out the Fry's Word list on page 74. It's worth its weight in gold.)

**Activities:** This segment offers you fun ideas to do together with your child. Many of the ideas are ideal for toddlers and older children, but don't underestimate your newborn! The activities are all centered around the daily topic and will help you get the whole family working together to verbalize as much as possible throughout the day through meaningful interaction.

(Note: Some activities are more easily done with toddlers and older children, but if you only have an infant or small toddler, just modify the activities so you can still do it with your baby and you are the one doing the talking.)

**Resources:** Finally, we have also included a list of resources you can use to enhance your daily talking. Each resource corresponds directly to the topic of the day and may include books, movies, and more. One great way to get some of the resources is to go to the library once a week and take home as many of the books on the list as possible. If the library is missing some they will be able to recommend other great books as a substitute.

In closing, it is important to note a few tips and pointers on how to make your talk time more effective.

### Good Talk vs. Bad Talk

1. Not all talking is equal. "Instruction-speak" (ie., sit down, be quiet, mind your manners) does little to help your child learn language. They need more in-depth discussions.

2. Negative talking (no, you can't, don't, etc.) is not helpful either. It is important to use uplifting, encouraging language. For every "no" your child hears, he should hear at least six words of encouragement and support

3. Baby talk vs. Adult talk - the best way to talk to your child to develop vocabulary and literacy is to talk to them like you do to other adults. Avoid baby talk. Just use your normal voice.

4. Questions - ask them questions! Of course they can't respond yet but that doesn't mean their brains aren't working and processing. Ask them, "How do you feel about this or that? What do you think?" Get their brains analyzing, thinking, and working on discovering their own thoughts and feelings.

5. Finally, fighting, arguing, and anger are not a productive means of teaching your child. We all get upset, so when it happens, try to keep your mouth closed. Put yourself in time out until you cool down. Remember, kids learn fast, and they tend to learn things we don't want them to! Be careful you aren't the one teaching them those things. The way you talk to them is how they will one day talk to you.

# Cost Benefit

Most early childhood development programs cost hundreds of dollars. Special childhood development toys are extremely expensive compared to their counterparts.

In comparison, this book and the knowledge it teaches costs

as little as $4.95 for the Kindle version. You can have that book with you every single day, wherever you go, so that you and your baby ALWAYS have something new to talk about and explore.

(NOTE: When you buy the printed version of the book from Amazon, you can also download the Kindle version for FREE. We also offer an online "digital" subscription - a whole year of Child Genius topics emailed straight to your inbox - a new one every day - for just $19.95.)

Of course it's possible for many parents to put together similar topics for days like we have done here, but the hours of time and effort it takes to do it well means that most parents will stop doing it long before they should. (The optimal implementation of the Child Genius 101 series is to use all 12 series - 365 topics - in a year, and then do that 3 more times, from birth through three years of age.)

We hope our efforts in gathering and compiling this information will help make it easier and more affordable for you and your children to talk, Talk, TALK and read, Read, READ!

# Conclusion

Although the original research behind this book was completed almost 20 years ago, the findings were so groundbreaking that the study continues to be used today in the academic field.

Unfortunately, there has been little in the way of implementation. Almost no one is educating new parents on the powerful concepts learned from that research. And even when they are educating parents, virtually no one provides simple, helpful resources to help the parent implement the findings.

Child Genius 101 does just that. It gives you the education to understand *WHY* talking and reading to your child are so critically important, and it gives you the daily resources to *MAKE IT EASY* to do.

The easier it is to do something, the more likely it is you'll do it. Actually getting in and doing the day-to-day work presented here won't always be easy. But it will be easier. And it is the most important work you could be doing for your new baby.

A Child Genius ***IS*** possible. Your actions each and every day ***WILL*** have a direct impact on your baby's IQ. We are honored to be a part of helping you and your child achieve your best, together!

# Apples

**TALK TIME:**

1. Tell your child about all the different varieties of apples you can find at a grocery store, farmers market, or apple-picking farm. (Macintosh, Pink Lady, Gala, Fuji, Red Delicious, Granny Smith).

2. Next describe all of the different uses for apples. Describe apples for baking things like apple pie or apple crumble. Talk about applesauce, caramel apples, and apple juice.

3. Describe the shape and color of different apples. If your family has a special or unique way of using apples, tell your child about this.

4. Talk to your child about the steps an apple takes from seed to tree, to picking and purchasing.

**QUESTIONS:**

1. Do you like apples?

2. Can you find an apple in your house?

3. What color is the apple you found?

4. What is your favorite apple?

5. What is your favorite recipe made with apples?

6. Have you played a game with apples before?

**VOCABULARY WORDS:**

apples, applesauce, apple seeds, apple pie, apple crisp, apple juice, apple-picking, apple tree, Macintosh, Pink Lady, Gala, Fuji, Red Delicious, Granny Smith, apple farm, farmers market, apple blossoms, caramel apples, sweet, sour, crunchy, mushy, ripe, rotten, worms

## ACTIVITIES:

1. Pick a recipe to make with your child that involves using apples as an ingredient. Read through the recipe together. Gather the ingredients and talk about them, or, better yet, make the recipe and talk about it while you work.

2. Check local farms that offer apple picking, viewing apple blossoms, or a farmers market that offers purchasing apple items and take your child with you to explore.

3. Plan a trip to the grocery store and allow your child to pick out one of each type of apple. Then plan a time at home to sample each apple and talk about the differences in taste.

## RESOURCES:

1. *Apple Fractions* by Jerry Pallota (Cartwheel, 2003)

2. *The Apple Pie* Tree by Zoe Hall (Blue Sky Press, 1996)

3. *Apples, Apples, Apples* by Nancy Elizabeth Wallace (Two Lions, 2004)

4. *The Biggest Apple Ever* by Steven Kroll (Cartwheel Books, 2011)

# Awards

**TALK TIME:**

1. Describe any awards or honors you received while attending grade school through high school. What did you have to do to earn the reward? Was it a trophy, medal, or certificate? Do you still have the award?

2. Did you receive any honors from places outside of school such as Boy/Girl Scouts, 4-H, or from sports teams? Did these awards mean more or less to you than school awards?

3. Talk about what it is like to be humble and show gratitude when accepting honors and awards. Did any of your awards open doors for you for future development, jobs, or new competitions?

4. Describe any team awards or honors you received and explain how these felt different from receiving individual rewards. These could be from participating in sports, debate, math club, chess club, etc.

**QUESTIONS:**

1. If you could give yourself a trophy, what would it be for?

2. How do you think you would behave if someone was giving you an award?

3. Are you on any teams now that are hoping to achieve an award or honors?

4. What kind of awards have you received in the past? What awards would you like to receive in the future?

**VOCABULARY WORDS:**

trophy, medal, certificate, ribbon, honor, humility, gratitude, effort, achievement, congratulations, recognition, success, failure, promotion, winning, winner, losing, loser, reward, championship, pinnacle, first place, runner-up, ability, strength, effort, training, intelligence

**ACTIVITIES:**

1. Make an award for each person and pet in the family with your child. Help them brainstorm the reason for each award. Next, have your child present the awards to each member during a special awards dinner. Have your child assist you with picking what the award dinner will be. Plan to give your child an award at the end as a surprise.

2. Get your child involved in house chores. Sit down with your child and create a board of things they can help with, such as taking their plate to the sink, making their bed, and feeding the dog.

Determine how many stars they need to gain an award. An award can be any number of things. It can be a piece of candy, a new book, or picking out the movie for the weekend.

**RESOURCES:**

1. *Sally Sore Loser: A Story About Winning and Losing* by Frank J. Sileo (Magination Press, 2012)

2. *Sam is Not a Loser* by Thierry Robberecht (Clarion Book, 2008)

3. *You Are Special* by Max Lucado (Crossway, 1997)

# Baseball

**TALK TIME:**

1. What is baseball? What are the rules? How is it played? Describe the game to your child in as much detail as you can. Talk about the pitcher, the batter, the outfielders, their positions, the innings, and any other elements of the game.

2. Did you ever play baseball as a child? Do you have any memories about playing with friends or family? Share those memories with your child. What position did you play? What was your team name? What parts of the game were you good at?

3. Do you know anything about the history of baseball you can share with your child? Or perhaps some of the players names or local team names?

4. If you don't care for baseball, tell your child why! Express your feelings and memories associated with the reason why you don't like baseball.

**QUESTIONS:**

1. What is name of the person who throws the ball?

2. What is your favorite thing about baseball?

3. Is a baseball easy or hard to throw?

**VOCABULARY WORDS:**

baseball, bat, catcher, pitcher, mound, batter, bases, innings, outfield, home run, bunt, national anthem, hot dogs, ball game, ball cap, helmet, uniform, team, sports, sportsmanship, play, work, train, practice

**ACTIVITIES:**

1. Play a game of paper baseball. Grab a few pieces of paper and some tape. Have your child help you make the paper into a ball and then use a few long strips of tape to secure it. Then use an empty paper towel roll for a bat, or for a challenge use a toilet paper roll. Make use of indoor and outdoor space, locate bases, and play ball!

2. Stay Home at the Ball Game! Cook up some hot dogs, slather on condiments, grab a soda pop, and watch a baseball game on television. During the off-season, watch a baseball movie. For dessert, try peanuts or popcorn. Be sure to cheer when they hit a home run!

3. Check out a minor league team in your city. Tickets are much more cost effective than a major league game, and they are set up to better cater to young ones.

**RESOURCES:**

1. *Little Baseball* by Brad Herzog (Sleeping Bear Press, 2011)

2. *The Berenstain Bears Go Out for the Team* by Stan Berenstain (Random House for Young Readers, 1987)

3. *The Littlest Leaguer* by Syd Hoff (HarperCollins, 2008)

4. DVD - *Everyone's Hero* (20th Century Fox, 2006)

5. DVD - *The Sandlot* (20th Century Fox, 1993)

6. DVD - *Rookie of the Year* (20th Century Fox, 1993)

# Blankets

## TALK TIME:

1. Did you have a favorite blanket as a child? If so, describe to your child what it looked like, how it made you feel, and what you liked about it. Tell your child where that blanket is now.

2. If your child has a special blanket, explain to them how you went about picking it out or making the blanket. Maybe the blanket was a gift from a family member or friend. Talk about how that makes it important.

3. Discuss the different textures and types of blankets--hand sewn, quilt, knit, store bought, fleece, thick or thin, fuzzy, wool, comforters, small blankets, big blankets, colors and patterns. Discuss how a blanket keeps you warm when you cover up in it.

## QUESTIONS:

1. Can you find a blanket?

2. Do you have a favorite blanket? How does it make you feel? Why is it your favorite?

3. Do your toys/dolls or family pets have blankets?

4. How can use blankets to make a fort?

5. What is the best color for a blanket?

6. Have you kept warm with something other than a blanket? What was it?

## VOCABULARY WORDS:

blanket, textures, comforter, colors, warmth, comfort, bed, hand sewn, quilt, knit, fleece, fuzzy, wool, soft, cozy, fabric, patterns, thick, thin, worn, tattered, stuffing, filler

## ACTIVITIES:

1. Round up all the blankets in the house. Use them to create forts, tunnels, the setting for a picnic, or for looking at the stars at night. Try a family movie night--pile up blankets on the floor and make some popcorn.

2. Check your local community center websites to see if any parks are hosting outdoor movies or free concerts for the summer. Grab a blanket and take your child to the kid-friendly show.

3. Plan a trip to your local fabric store. Look at the different patterns and textures. Feel as many fabrics as possible and talk about what makes each one unique. If possible, pick out a favorite and take it home to make it into a blanket.

## EASY FLEECE BLANKET DIRECTIONS:

1. Take two fabric pieces equal in size and line them up (no stuffing/filler required). Every half inch, snip 2 to 3 inches into the fabric. Next tie each side of the lose fabric together like a knot. Work all the way around. When you are finished, you will have a secure and cozy machine-washable blanket.

## RESOURCES:

1. *Baby Duck and the Cozy Blanket* (Touch and Feel) by Amy Hest (Candlewick, 2002)

2. *Pigs on a Blanket* by Amy Axelrod (Aladdin, 1998)

3. DVD - *Happiness is a Warm Blanket*, Charlie Brown (Warner Home Video, 2011) DVD - The Sandlot (20th Century Fox, 1993)

# Boxes

## TALK TIME:

1. Explain the shape of the box or boxes you have chosen to show your child. Are they long and rectangular or perfectly square on all sides like a cube?

2. Talk about the material boxes are made with. Cheap boxes are usually made of corrugated layers of cardboard, and some that are nicer might be made with plastic or covered in leather or fabric.

3. Tell your child what the boxes you have are used for. Talk about what big boxes are used for and what smaller ones are used for. Think about lunch boxes, toolboxes, and food boxes. Talk about boxes you have received or boxes you have sent in the mail. Share with your little one memories of opening gifts in boxes and what was inside them.

## QUESTIONS:

1. What shape is this box?

2. What is this box made of?

3. What do you do with boxes?

4. Can you count the side of a box?

## VOCABULARY WORDS:

corner, plane, box, leather, cardboard, material, texture, fold, bend, open, close, top, lid, inside, outside, upside-down, around, stiff, soft, hard, sturdy, weak, small, large, gift, mail, rectangle, square, trapezoid, rhombus, polygon, quadrilateral

**ACTIVITIES:**

1. Grab some empty boxes from the kitchen recycle bin (cereal boxes, pasta boxes, mac and cheese boxes). Have your child use them as blocks to build or draw on them. Have your child trace words and pictures on the box. Ask your child what they can use the box for--drum, boxcar, hat? What else?

2. Play! Let your child climb in and around and inside of a box (if you have one big enough). Let your child take the lid off and on the box or move the flaps that open and close. As your child plays, say the terms that describe where your child is in relation the box.

3. Grab some paper and have your child draw boxes. Experiment with color and size. How many boxes can your child fit on one page?

4. Box hunt count. Have your child hunt their room for boxes. How many can they find? Have them count.

5. Make a box-only meal. With your child's help, have a meal using only foods and drinks from boxes. Think juice boxes, lasagna, and ice cream sandwiches.

**RESOURCES:**

1. *A Box Can Be Many Things* by Dana Meachen Rau (Children's Press, 1997)

2. *A Box Story* by Kenneth Kit Lamug (Rabblebox, 2011)

3. *My Box Book* by Will Hillenbrand (Harcourt Children's Books, 2006)

4. *Not a Box* by Antoinette Portis (HarperCollins, 2006)

# Bugs!

**TALK TIME:**

1. Tell your child everything you know about bugs, insects and arachnids. Spiders, beetles, mosquitoes, dragonflies, bees, butterflies, and cockroaches! What other bugs can you tell your child about? Be sure to describe what they look like, where they live, and what they do. Do they fly? Walk? Swim?

2. If you know the differences between bugs, insects and arachnids, tell your child. If not, no biggie. Just tell them as much as you know, or look up the differences so you can explain it better. (Hint: arachnids have eight legs, and all bugs are insects, but not all insects are bugs).

3. How do you feel about insects? Talk about your emotions and feelings as they relate to all sorts of different insects. Butterflies probably make you feel vastly different than flying grasshoppers, right? And how about those arachnids, like black widow spiders?

4. What's the worst memory you ever had with bugs? Share the story with your child. (At this point, don't worry about scaring her. She's too small to understand that side of things. Just be careful that you don't communicate fear as you speak and you'll be fine. She's paying more attention to the words right now, but she will definitely pick up on your emotional cues as well.)

5. What kinds of bugs are useful for humans (bees and silkworms are a good example). Why else are bugs important to humans? Talk about the "circle of life" and how everything eats something, and the fact that there are billions and trillions of bugs buzzing and crawling around the world means that all the animals and plants get to eat, be pollinated and grow, so in turn we can eat the food that comes from them.

**QUESTIONS:**

1. What does a bug feel like when it crawls on your hand?

2. What insect, bug or arachnid do you like the least?

3. Do you have a favorite bug?

## VOCABULARY WORDS:

bugs, insects, arachnids, ladybug, spider, grasshopper, bee, butterfly, dragonfly, beetle, scorpion, firefly, snail, ant, cockroach, worms, small, exoskeleton

## ACTIVITIES:

1. You don't need a magnifying glass to look for bugs, just some focused searching. Take your child on a walk around the backyard or at the park. Look under picnic tables, around plants, or chairs.

2. Ready, set, draw! How many different bugs can your child draw in five minutes?

3. Try a new kind of butterfly artwork. Ask your child what bug they think would be better than a caterpillar that could change into a butterfly. Have them draw what their version would look like.

4. Surprise your child with a movie night and some creepy crawly gummy worms to munch. Or how about some honey sticks (opening up a discussion of bees).

## RESOURCES:

1. *Bugs!* by David T. Greenberg (Little Brown Books for Young Readers, 2002)

2. *Bugs Galore* by Peter Stein (Candlewick, 2012)

3. *I Like Bugs* by Margaret Wise Brown (Random House Books for Young Readers, 1999)

4. DVD - *A Bug's Life* (Disney-Pixar, 1998)

5. DVD - *The Fascinating World of Insects* (BrainFood Learning 2011)

# Camping

**TALK TIME:**

1. Discuss the things that you enjoy most about camping. Is it the trip to reach the camping destination or is it the camping itself? Talk about going somewhere new and meeting new people. Tell your child about your most memorable camping trip experience.

2. Talk about the foods that you eat when you go camping--roasting marshmallows and making s'mores, grilling hot dogs and hamburgers, or cooking fresh fish from the lake.

3. Discuss the places where you have been camping and where you hope to go camping in the future. Is it in the backyard, at parks, campgrounds, beach, lake, or in the woods?

4. Discuss the animals or insects you heard or saw while you were camping. Talk about the clothing you have to wear for camping.

5. Tell funny stories about setting up a tent, dealing with a sleeping bag zipper that got stuck, or adventures with the flashlight in the middle of the night.

**QUESTIONS:**

1. Do you like camping?

2. What animals do you think you would see when camping?

3. What activities do you do when camping?

4. Can you name three different places where you could go camping?

5. What do you miss most about home when you are camping?

**VOCABULARY WORDS:**

camping, tent, pitch, nature, campfire, hiking, trail, flashlight, zipper, sleeping bag, destination, experience, grilling, hot dogs, hamburgers, wood, mountains, forest, fir trees, lake, river, stream, dirt, dirty

**ACTIVITIES:**

1. Set up camp inside or outside. Bring all the items you would normally use when camping outdoors. If camping inside think of how you could make it special. Cook hot dogs or hamburgers, or make some cookies to take with you to your "camp spot." Leave all technology devices inside or turned off. Enjoy telling stories around the "campfire" and looking at the stars.

2. Go on a camping walk. Point out items you might see during a real camping trip. Don't be afraid to pretend! Have your child take a flashlight and explore.

3. Grab some paper and crayons or even your computer's paint program. Have your child draw their vision of the perfect campsite, including who they would invite and what items they would bring.

4. Not enough time to camp? Roast marshmallows for s'mores!

**S'MORES RECIPE (in the microwave):**

Take half a graham cracker and a chocolate square, and stick a marshmallow on top. Microwave for about 15-20 seconds, depending on microwave. Have your child watch the marshmallow puff up. Carefully remove, place other graham cracker on top, and enjoy!

**RESOURCES:**

1. *Curious George Goes Camping* by Margaret Ray (HMH Books, 1999)

2. *Fred and Ted Go Camping* by Peter Eastman (Random House Books for Young Readers, 2005)

3. *Just Me and My Dad* by Mercer Mayer (Random House Books for Young Readers, 2001)

4. DVD - *Camp Nowhere* (Walt Disney Video/Mill Creek, 1994)

5. DVD - *Race For Your Life*, Charlie Brown (Paramount, 1977)

# Castles

**TALK TIME:**

1. Tell your child where castles can be found. England, Germany, and Ireland are just a few places castles can be found. Castles can even be found in the United States.

2. Explain the massive size of a castle. Describe characteristics of a castle, such as moats, stone construction, small windows, high walls, battlements, draw bridges, towers, and gateways.

3. Talk about stories that feature castles in them, such as Rapunzel. Discuss how she had let her long hair down from the castle window.

4. Discuss that castles were built to protect the surrounding villages and used as defensive structures. Tell your child that castles started to appear in the world in the early 10th century.

**QUESTIONS:**

1. What castles can you name?

2. Would you live in a castle? What name would you call your castle?

3. Do you think castles are dark and scary or big and adventurous?

**VOCABULARY WORDS:**

castle, 10th century, Rapunzel, moats, stone construction, Harry Potter, battlements, draw bridges, towers, gateways, England, Germany, Ireland, United States castles, defense, protection, dim light, spacious, king, queen, prince, princess, knight, royalty, peasants, medieval

**ACTIVITIES:**

1. Search the Internet for images of castles. Have a discussion with your child about what they see. Next have your child draw a picture of a castle, or draw one for them.

2. Check your state's website. Are there castles within an hour drive? You don't have to spend money on a tour. Simply view the outside and ask your child what they think is inside.

3. Does the local park or mall have a castle in the play area? If so, go check it out.

4. Allow your child to make their bed into a castle. Incorporate pillows, blankets, and chairs to add a moat. Create passwords to allow entry into the castle. What does your child see out the windows once they are in the pretend castle?

**RESOURCES:**

1. *A Year in a Castle* by Rachel Coombs (First Avenue Editions, 2009)

2. *The Secret of Terror Castles* (The Three Investigators #1) by Robert Arthur (Random House Books for Young Readers, 1991)

3. *Bob the Builder: The Knights of Fix-a-Lot* (a DVD movie about fixing a castle)

4. Check out documentaries available from A&E on castles.

5. Harry Potter castle puzzles, as well as other puzzles of castles.

# Dessert

**TALK TIME:**

1. Talk to your child about different types of desserts. Describe desserts that are most enjoyed in the summer months, and those most enjoyed in the winter months.

2. Discuss holidays, special occasion desserts, or a culture or family dessert. Is there a special family dessert that is only made by memory? Explain what the dessert is and what makes it special.

3. Describe to your child what your favorite dessert is and why. Tell your child if you had rules in your house as a child about eating your dinner before you could have dessert.

4. Discuss how desserts can be many different things--some can be non-traditional or even healthy and sugar-free

**QUESTIONS:**

1. Have you ever had a dessert you didn't like?

2. Do you wish you could have dessert every night?

3. Do you have to finish all your dinner to have dessert?

4. What are your favorite desserts? What are your least favorite?

**VOCABULARY WORDS:**

dessert, ice cream, cake, candy, chocolate, cookies, pie, holiday desserts, family desserts, cultural desserts, non-traditional desserts, summer desserts, winter desserts, healthy desserts, sugar-free desserts, frosting, sprinkles, honey, agave, artificial sweetener, sweet, sugar, fat, carbohydrates, energy

**ACTIVITIES:**

1. Take a trip to the grocery store and have your child pick out ice cream, sprinkles, chocolate and anything else they want to make a sundae.

2. Take out the blender and make a fruit shake using honey or agave as a sweetener.

3. Grab some old magazines, paper, glue and scissors. Have your child cut out pictures of dessert items to make a collage.

4. Find a family recipe or a brand new dessert recipe to make with your child. It could even be something simple, such as Rice Crispy Treats.

5. Just dessert. Head over to a local restaurant just to order dessert with your child or entire family.

**RESOURCES:**

1. *Chocolate Chill-Out Cake and Other Yummy Desserts* by Nick Fauchald (Picture Window Books, 2008)

2. *If You Give a Mouse a Cookie* by Laura Joffe Numeroff (HarperCollins, 2010) or If You Give a Cat a Cupcake (HarperCollins, 2008)

3. *Little Pea* by Amy Krouse Rosenthal (Chronicle Books, 2005)

# Dogs

**TALK TIME:**

1. Did you have any dogs when you were a child? Share a story from your childhood about a dog you had or a dog you remember. What color was it? Describe the breed. How old were you? What was the dog's name? What sort of things did you do together?

2. Have you ever had a dog that you didn't like? Why didn't you like it? Tell your child all the same details as above about this dog too.

3. What is a dog? Talk about what makes a dog a dog! A wagging tail, a panting tongue, claws that don't retract, etc. Talk about the ears, the eyes, the nose (and how its sense of smell is better than human noses).

4. What kinds of dogs are there? What different breeds can you tell your child about? German Shepherd, Golden Retriever, Beagle, Rottweiler, Doberman Pincer, Alaskan Malamute, Collie, even mixed breeds.

5. Where did dogs come from? Talk about wolves and how dogs are descendants of wolves. Talk about where wolves live. What do they eat and how do they hunt?

6. Dogs are very social animals. Like wolves, they like to live in packs. Talk about how your family can be a pack for a dog, or if you don't have a dog, how your family can be a pack for each other.

**QUESTIONS:**

1. If you don't have a dog would you want to have a dog?

2. If you have a dog is your dog big or small? If you don't, would you like a big or small dog?

3. What does a dog's hair feel like?

4. What do you call a dog's feet?

5. Is a dog bigger or smaller than a horse?

6. What noises does a dog make?

**VOCABULARY WORDS:**

dog, paws, ears, nose, tail, teeth, Labradors, Doberman, Beagle, Poodle, Terrier, Greyhound, Mastiff, Collie, dog food, dog toys, collar, licking, bark, whine, growl, tricks, obedient, roll over, play dead, sit, stay

**ACTIVITIES:**

1. Take a trip to the local dog shelter or a local dog rescue home and see if they could use a volunteer for a few hours. Use the volunteer opportunity to spend quality time with your child.

2. The perfect dog. Have your child draw their idea of the perfect dog. Have them draw the dog and what it would eat. What would its bed look like? What toys would it play with?

3. Dog shapes. Create a dog out of shapes. Cut out shapes that would work for your child to create a dog face. Glue to a paper plate or to an empty toilet paper roll.

4. Make a homemade dog storybook. Have your child come up with a beginning, middle, and ending to a story about a dog. Cut and staple paper to make a book. Have your child draw pictures as you write what your child tells you is happening on each page.

**RESOURCES:**

1. *Busy Doggies* by John Schindel (Tricycle Press, 2003)

2. *Digby Takes Charge* by Caroline Jayne Church (Margaret K. McElderry Books, 2007)

3. *If You Give a Dog a Donut* by Laura Numeroff (Balzer & Bray, 2011)

4. DVD - *Because of Winn-Dixie* (20th Century Fox. The book by Kate DiCamillo is available from Candlewick Press, 2000)

5. DVD - *Homeward Bound* and *Homeward Bound II* (Walt Disney Home Video, 1993 and 1996)

# Elephants

**TALK TIME:**

1. Discuss with your child where elephants live other than the zoo. Talk about Africa and Asia and how the elephants from each country have differences in their head and ear shapes.

2. What types of food do elephants eat and how do they eat these foods? How do elephants drink water?

3. Discuss how an elephant stays cool In the heat by covering themselves in the cool mud or spraying themselves with water from a waterhole.

4. For an elephant that lives at the zoo discuss how a zookeeper cares for the elephant. For an elephant that lives in the wild, discuss how elephants care for their family.

5. Discuss the parts of an elephant such as the tusks, trunk, tail, and ears. Talk about the gray sun-soaked skin and the big feet and toenails elephants have.

6. Tell your child about seeing an elephant for the first time. Did you like them or were you scared by their massive size?

**QUESTIONS:**

1. What is the most interesting part of an elephant?

2. What do you think an elephant's skin feels like? Soft? Rough?

3. Do you think an elephant likes to live in the zoo or in the wild?

4. How do elephants eat?

5. Name the different parts of an elephant and then move around like an elephant.

6. What is the difference between an African elephant and Asian elephant (hint: ears and head)?

## VOCABULARY WORDS:

elephant, mammal, tusks, weapons, trunk, zoo, mud, waterhole, Asia, Africa, continent, terrestrial animals, savannahs, herbivores, marshes, ivory, peanuts, peanut butter, spray, tail, ears, massive, heavy, large, migrate, mammoth, mastodon, extinct

## ACTIVITIES:

1. Have a scavenger hunt for peanuts. Then have your child walk like an elephant and smell for the peanuts with their pretend trunk to find the hidden peanuts.

2. Eat like an elephant at the zoo! Have a plate full of apples, bananas, pears and some peanut butter for dipping. (Elephants also eat vegetables, but those don't taste good dipped in peanut butter.)

3. Summer Time: With the water hose, kiddie pool, or big pool, try cooling yourself off like an elephant with its trunk.

4. Take a trip to your local zoo and observe the elephants, or if there isn't one close, look up some videos about elephants on the internet.

## RESOURCES:

1. *But No Elephants* by Jerry Smath (CQ Products, 2007)

2. *Elephants Cannot Dance* (part of the Piggie and Elephant series) by Mo Willems (Hyperion Book, 2009)

3. *"Stand Back," Said the Elephant, "I'm Going to Sneeze!"* by Patricia Thomas (Lothrop, Lee & Shepard Books, 1990)

4. *Babar* books by Jean De Brunhoff (Random House) as well as the Babar movies.

# Fruit

**TALK TIME:**

1. What is your favorite fruit? Describe it – how it looks, how it smells, how it feels, and how it tastes. Why is it your favorite? How long has it been your favorite?

2. Name as many fruits as you can: Apples, bananas, strawberries, grapefruit, lemon, lime, orange, tangerine, blueberries, raspberries, grapes, pineapple, etc. Tell your child about each one. Where do they come from--trees or ground plants? Talk about the different kinds of foods you can prepare with these fruits or your favorite ways to eat them.

3. What is your favorite memory about fruit? Or maybe your worst memory? Are there any fruits you don't like or are allergic to?

4. Talk about a social gathering you had recently where you ate fruit. Discuss what fruits were there.

5. Why is fruit an important part of our diets? You might want to talk about complex carbohydrates and complex sugars verses refined white sugar.

6. Have you ever grown fruit on your own? Tell your child about your gardening experience. Have you ever seen bananas, oranges, or some other fruit growing on a tree? Where were you?

**QUESTIONS:**

1. What color is a lemon?

2. What do oranges taste like?

3. Do you like eating fruits?

4. How many fruits can you name?

5. What is your favorite and least favorite fruit?

6. What fruits do you think would taste good together?

## VOCABULARY WORDS:

fruit, orange, apple, sour, sweet, citrus, tart, bright colors, fresh, produce, planting, fruit trees, cut, juice, peel, crisp, soft, blend, chop, eat, diet, nutrients, vitamins, minerals, health, body, meal, dish, recipe, fruit tray, dip, finger food, fruit salad, preparation

## ACTIVITIES:

1. Head to the grocery store with your child and pick out only fruit. Don't be afraid to get fruits that you might have never tried before. Once at home, wash, cut and do fruit taste-testing. For the fruits your child already knows, try blindfolding and see if they can guess what they are eating without looking.

2. Make a recipe with fruit in it with your child. Or try a fruit smoothie, experimenting with different fruits, incorporating math through measuring cups.

3. Check your local area for fruit picking, or with your older kids try making/canning jam. Instructions can easily be located on the Internet.

**RECIPE:** fruit smoothie for the blender

1 cup strawberries
1 cup blueberries
½ cup of plain yogurt/strawberry or blueberry
3 tablespoons of honey or agave
1 cup ice

## RESOURCES:

1. *Fruits I Love* by Victoria Boutenko (Raw Family, 2011)

2. *The Little Mouse, The Red Ripe Strawberry, The Big Hungry Bear by Don Wood* (Child's Play, 1997)

3. *Touch and feel book, I Like Fruit: Petit Collage* by Lorena Siminovich (Templar; Brdbk edition, 2010)

# Goals & Dreams

**TALK TIME:**

1. Tell your child about some of your lifetime goals. Do you have fitness goals? Financial goals? Dreams to travel to far off places? Aspirations to become a famous author? Explore some of your goals in detail with your child.

2. What is the difference between a goal and a dream? Explain how goals are things we work on consistently (the more often the better) whereas dreams are things we don't have a lot of influence on, we just hope they will happen.

3. What are some of the goals you have already accomplished in life? Talk about each one and explain the steps and process you went through in order to achieve the goals.

4. What's your philosophy about goal-setting? What did your parents teach you about goal-setting, either by example or by word?

5. Feel free to set new goals with your child today. For example, you could proactively talk to your child each day, hint, hint! Explain how goals and dreams can change over time and express how that is a good thing.

**QUESTIONS:**

1. Do you have a dream?

2. Would you like to make a goal?

3. Is there a goal we can make together?

4. What are some of your biggest goals in life?

5. What are some dreams you have seen other people accomplish? How do you think they felt after accomplishing that goal?

## VOCABULARY WORDS:

goal, dream, aspiration, dedication, perspiration, driven, determination, hard work, one day at a time, freedom, fit, fitness, strong, health, wealthy, financial independence, home, house, travel, beach, island, ocean, airplane, love, happiness, satisfaction, bliss

## ACTIVITIES:

1. Explore different local venues and events so your child can see other's goals and dreams in action. Try going to a local art show or farmer's market. Engage and encourage your child to ask questions such as why an artist became an artist, or why a baker became a baker.

2. Search your local city recreation department and see what events/classes/groups are available to your child that might assist in a deeper understanding of goals and dreams.

3. Include your child in house chores, cooking, and shopping so that your child can discover the things they like and don't like, as well as what they are good at.

4. For older kids, have your child start a journal. Encourage them to write down their goals and dreams. Remind them that they can change or add to their dreams at anytime.

## RESOURCES:

1. *Oh the Places You Will Go* by Dr. Seuss (Random House, 1990)

2. DVD - *Rudy* (Sony Pictures Home Entertainment, 1993)

3. DVD - *Space Jam* (Warner Home Video,1996)

4. DVD - *The Blind Side* (Warner Home Video, 2009)

# Instruments

**TALK TIME:**

1. Tell your child about an instrument you played in school. Discuss what you liked or didn't like about the instrument. If you didn't play an instrument explain why.

2. Discuss the different types instruments--brass, woodwinds, strings, percussion, keyboard and electric. Talk about what makes them different or similar.

3. Have fun making noises with your mouth or hands and explain how those can be instruments too. Discuss how Tupperware, paper towel rolls, pots and pans, and spoons forks and knives can all be used to make music. Now go make some!

4. Discuss bands and orchestras and how instruments come together to make music. Talk about the conductor and how a conductor makes sure the instruments flow together.

**QUESTIONS:**

1. Can an animal play an instrument?

2. Can you stomp your feet? You just made a rhythm.

3. If you don't play an instrument, would you like to? If you do play an instrument why did you pick that one?

4. What is your favorite instrument?

5. What is your least favorite?

**VOCABULARY WORDS:**

drum, violin, tuba, accordion, brass, cello, flute, piano, keyboard, electric guitar, guitar, music, instruments, homemade instruments, woodwinds, orchestra, conductor, sound, timber, key, pedal, string, strum, pluck, pick, blow, sound wave, music, harmony, chord, melody

**ACTIVITIES:**

1. Have some fun with your child searching for items in your house to make homemade instruments. Once several items have been located, experiment with rhythm and soft and louder sounds.

2. After the experimenting is over, maybe your child would like to put on a concert for the family with their new homemade instruments.

3. Check out your local library for CD's that focus on instrumental music. Play the CD and see if your child can pick out which instrument is playing at any given time.

**RESOURCES:**

1. *I Know a Shy Fellow Who Swallowed a Cello* by Barbara Garriel (Boyds Mills Press, 2004)

2. *Meet the Orchestra* by Ann Hayes (Sandpiper, 1995)

3. Click on over to Sphinx Kids! at http://www.sphinxkids.org/ for an assortment of fun instrument based games for kids.

# Laundry

**TALK TIME:**

1. Explain to your child why it is important to keep clothes clean. Talk about how you know when an item of clothing needs to go through the wash, like if it has visible stains or if it smells bad.

2. Now talk about how you organize the clothes that need to be washed. How do you gather the clothes for washing? Does everyone in the house have a laundry basket they keep dirty clothes in? Do you separate different colors and fabric-types into piles before washing?

3. Share with your child your methods of washing your clothes. If you use a machine, talk about the settings you use and what kind of soap you add. If you hand wash, talk about how the soap is used and why you hand wash the clothes. Or, if you use dry-cleaning or go to a Laundromat, talk about that, as well.

4. Next explain to your child how you dry the clothes after they have been washed and rinsed. Do you use a dryer, hang dry, or iron the clothing? Talk about how an iron works, as well as how to safely use an iron.

5. Take a final moment to talk about how you fold and put the clothes away. Tell your child where you store clothes—do you hang them in a closet, place them in drawers, or keep them on a shelf somewhere? Maybe they get piled on a table for family members to grab or left in the dryer.

**QUESTIONS:**

1. Why do we wash our clothes?

2. How do we wash the clothes?

3. Does the dryer use hot or cold air to dry the clothing? Or both?

4. What would happen if we never washed our clothes?

5. Do you like the smell of clean clothes? Why?

**VOCABULARY WORDS:**

wash, clean, laundry, clothes, fabrics, soft, rough, smooth, silk, worn, tattered, starch, fabric softener, soap, detergent, settings, dial, buttons, machine, scrub, soak, hot water, stains, stain-remover, spray, press, iron, steam, dry, hang, pins, clothes-line, drip-dry, hand-wash

**ACTIVITIES:**

1. Have your child hand wash something small, like a washcloth. Allow them to take their time and have fun with the soap, scrubbing it. This can be done outside in a small plastic bin, in the bathroom sink, or better yet, in the tub!

2. Encourage your child to help you with the laundry. Start with sorting the colors, loading the machine, adding the soap, putting clothes in the dryer or hanging them on a line, and then finally folding them. If you go to the Laundromat have your child help with adding the money to start the machines.

3. Laundry toss. Grab a hamper and see from how far away your child can toss the laundry in. It can be something small like a sock or washcloth.

**RESOURCES:**

1. *A Pocket for Corduroy* by Don Freeman (Puffin, 2008)

2. *Doing the Washing* by Sarah Garland (Frances Lincoln Children's Books, 2009)

3. *Laundry Day* by Maurie J. Manning (Clarion Books, 2012)

4. *The Day Jimmy's Boa Ate the Wash* by Trinka Hakes Noble (Puffin, 1992)

# Leaves

**TALK TIME:**

1. Discuss a leaf's shape, texture, and color. Did you collect leaves as a child? If so, share your thoughts on fall leaves. Maybe there was a favorite story from your childhood that had leaves in it?

2. Discuss why leaves fall from the trees. Talk about how this happens when the weather cools and when their is less sunlight in the day. Explain how some trees change colors and lose their leaves and other trees do not.

3. If you have ever run, jumped, or hopped though a pile of leaves describe how this felt for you as a child. Describe the noise it made and how you had to help rake them up afterward.

4. Discuss how new leaves grow (re-growth) on tree branches when the weather warms up in the spring.

**QUESTIONS:**

1. What is your favorite thing about leaves?

2. Can you name something that is smaller than a leaf and bigger than a leaf?

3. Does a leaf fall fast or slow from the tree branch?

4. What types of trees/leaves are around outside of your home? If you have houseplants examine those leaves. What do you see?

5. Hold a leaf up to the light and examine the veins. What do you see?

6. Can you think of what trees lose their leaves in the fall? Which leaves turn color?

## VOCABULARY WORDS:

fall, leaf, tree, veins, stem, seasons, deciduous (a tree that loses its leaves), pine trees, needles, rake, colors, spring, growth, foliage, fruit trees, leaf art, cooking with leaves, basil, sage, mint, cilantro

## ACTIVITIES:

1. Spring, summer, or fall leaves are all around us, even wintertime for those in warmer climates. Take a walk outside and collect a few different ones. Grab some paint, and using items you have at home, paint the leaves and then use them as stamps on paper (try Q-tips or sponges to paint the leaves). Next try making a crayon or colored pencil rub with the paper on top of the leaf.

2. Head on over to the local home improvement store and pick out paint sample colors (fall or summer colors). Take them home to use for tracing and cutting leaves or free-hand drawing.

3. Have your child assist you when cooking something that has leaves. Many simple recipes have basil, cilantro, mint, or sage leaves in them.

## RESOURCES:

1. *A Leaf Can Be...* by Laura Purdie Salas (Millbook Press, 2012)

2. *Leaves* by David Ezra Stein (Putman Juvenile, 2007)

3. *Let it Fall* by Maryann Cocca-Leffler (Cartwell Books, 2010)

# Money

**TALK TIME:**

1. Tell your child what money is. Talk about coins and dollars, how they look, how they feel, etc. Feel free to even pull out some money and let your child look at it and feel it.

2. Tell your child about what you can do with money. Buy things, pay rent, pay bills, invest in stocks, loan it out, etc. Talk about all the things you do with your money each week. Talk about all the bills and expenses, such as groceries and utilities. Talk about spending some of the money on fun things like eating out or renting a movie.

3. How do you earn your money? Talk about how you are paid for the work you do. Talk about your boss, your co-workers, your responsibilities and duties at work, and all the things involved in how you earn your money.

4. Talk about your financial goals and/or challenges. Talk about the things you'd like to accomplish financially, like buying a house or taking a vacation.

**QUESTIONS:**

1. What would you like to buy with money?

2. How will you earn money when you grow up?

3. What will you save your money for?

4. What kind of jobs or work do you not want to do?

**VOCABULARY WORDS:**

money, cash, change, dollars, nickel, dime, quarter, penny, one, five, ten, twenty, one hundred, save, savings, checking, check, account, bank, invest, stock, mutual fund, rent, loan, payday, paycheck, taxes, insurance, finances, financial freedom, credit, debt, bankruptcy

**ACTIVITIES:**

1. Make your own play money. Have your child design, draw, and color their own set of currency. Allow them to use this created money to purchase items around the house for fun.

2. Take your child out to a Dollar Store and let them buy an item. If there is a family pet let your child pay for a new pet toy or treat.

3. Does your child have a piggy bank? Help them start saving. Older kids can open their own savings account watch their money start to grow. Start by having them save ten percent of their allowance.

4. Pretend restaurant. Have your child plan a menu. Assist your child with listing prices on the menu. Make sure that after ordering and enjoying dinner that your child pays the bill!

**RESOURCES:**

1. *Just Saving My Money* by Mercer Mayer (HarperCollins, 2010)

2. *Money, Money, Honey Bunny!* by Marilyn Sadler (Random House Books for Young Readers, 2006)

3. *The Berenstain Bears' Trouble with Money* by Stan Berenstain (Random House Books for Young Readers, 1983)

# Opposites

**TALK TIME:**

1. How would you define the word "opposite"? Think beyond big and small.

2. Now demonstrate what opposites are. You could easily show light and dark by letting your child flip the light switch on and off. Allow your child to touch something smooth and then something rough. Show as many opposites as you see around you by providing a hands-on experience.

3. Tell your child something that you like and don't like that would be an opposite. For example you like the house to be clean verses dirty. Maybe you like being tall verses being short. Maybe you like the night better than the day. Explain why you like one opposite over the other.

**QUESTIONS:**

1. (Using an object:) Is this object above or below the table?

2. How are you and I opposite?

3. (Using two objects:) Which one is bigger? Smaller?

**VOCABULARY WORDS:**

feel, touch, see, look, observe, examine, notice, difference, hold, big, little, small, tall, wide, short, flat, 3-dimensional, texture, rough, smooth, soft, delicate, hard, brush, grainy, light, heavy, dark, light, shapes, surfaces, colors, temperature, location, appearance, listen, watch

## ACTIVITIES:

1. Have your child identify some opposites around the house. Think about colors, light and dark, up and down, tall and short, wide and thin, front and back, open and closed, fast and slow, soft and hard. Just have fun with your little one and the things around you. You could even use your voice to demonstrate loud and quiet.

2. Prepare a meal with your child that has opposites of hot and cold, big and little.

3. Play an opposites match game. Cut a piece of paper into eight pieces. Have your child draw the same object - big on one paper and small on another. If needed, assist your child in drawing these pictures. Flip them over and play match.

4. Act out opposites. Take your child in your arms and demonstrate the opposite of up and down, in and out, sit and stand, fast and slow. Think of the fun ways you can be active with your child while you help them learn about opposites in action.

## RESOURCES:

1. *Duck and Goose – What's Up Duck?* (A Book of Opposites) by Tad Hills (Boxer Books Limited, 2010)

2. *Opposites* by Sandra Boynton (Little Simon, 1982)

3. *The Opposite* by Tom MacRae (Peachtree Publishers, 2006)

4. DVD - *Elmo's World: Opposites* (Sesame Street, 2010)

# Outer Space

**TALK TIME:**

1. What do you think of when you hear the words "outer space?" Planets, the sun, moon, stars, black holes, rockets, spaceships, aliens, etc. Talk about everything that comes to mind! Mars, Jupiter, Venus, Uranus, Pluto, Earth, etc.

2. What are your favorite movies about space? Who was in the movie? What was the plot? What do you remember most from the movie? (Men in Black, Apollo 13, WALL-E, Star Trek, Star Wars, Dune, and The Last Starfighter. (Leave out any scary descriptions depending on your child's age).

3. You can also talk about today's space programs: NASA, space exploration, Hubble telescope, astronauts, etc.

4. Talk about your beliefs about what is out there. Is there life on other planets? What is beyond the Milky Way? What do aliens look like?

**QUESTIONS:**

(Take your child outside. For younger ones, point out what you see. For older kids have them tell you what they see.)

1. What color is the sky?

2. Can you see the stars?

3. Do you want to go to space?

4. Can you find the moon?

**VOCABULARY WORDS:**

Space, galaxy, milky way, planets, moon, solar system, star, sun, universe, astronaut, astronomy, meteor, comet, orbit, constellations, gravity, lunar, sky, spaceship, outer space, rocket, blast off, shuttle, solar, lightyear, science fiction

## ACTIVITIES:

1. Set up an area to create a pretend spaceship. Use a bed or rope off an area with chairs or stuffed animals. Blast off into space. Once you are out in space, have your child tell you what they see--other planets, stars, etc.

2. Visit a local store that sells camping supplies. Often they have freeze dried foods (space food). Purchase one (ice cream is always a favorite) and take it back to the spaceship to taste while in outer space together.

3. Space drawing. Ask your child to draw what they think is in outer space. Remind them to think beyond the planets and stars. If your child is too young, you can draw what you think space looks like, talking to your child all the while about what you are drawing.

## RESOURCES:

1. *I Want to be an Astronaut* by Byron Barton (HarperCollins, 1992)

2. *If You Decide to go to the Moon* by Faith Mcnutly (Scholastic Press, 2005)

3. *Our Stars* by Anne Rockwell (Sandpiper, 2002)

4. DVD - *Flight of the Navigator* (Walt Disney, 1986)

5. DVD - *Mars Needs Moms* (Walt Disney Studios, 2011)

6. DVD - *Space Camp* (MGM, 1986)

# Painting

## TALK TIME:

1. What descriptive words would you use to describe paint to your child? Wet, goopy, smooth, cold, colorful?

2. Next, tell your child about the different types of paints you know about. Talk about oil paints, acrylic, watercolors, and spray-paints. What are the differences? What are the similarities? Have you ever painted with any of these paints on paper or a canvas? Think back to your art classes in school.

3. Have you ever painted the walls in your home or the exterior of your home? Maybe your little pinewood derby car back in Boy Scouts? Or maybe some sort of craft in Girl Scouts, or a birdhouse?

## QUESTIONS:

1. What is paint?

2. What does paint feel like on your fingers?

3. What can you do with paint?

4. What color of paint do you like the most?

## VOCABULARY WORDS:

pigment, material, medium, hues, shades, colors, mix, blend, oil paint, color wheel, fingers, brushes, canvas, art, crafts, watercolor, expression, picture, piece, surface, decorate

## ACTIVITIES:

1. Lay down an old bed sheet on the floor that you don't mind getting stained. Take it outside in the grass or driveway, or sit at a table with newspaper underneath. Put paint in small containers like the lid of a jar or on a paper plate. (There are many brands of child-safe, easy-

to-clean, stain-free paints.) Provide a piece of paper and let your child explore with paint, showing them how to use their fingers (or paint-brushes) to push the pigment across the surface.

2. Try Q-tip painting. Place several different colors in shallow containers or paper plates and provide a Q-tip for each color. Allow your child to explore the paper with the paint-covered Q-tip.

3. Do you have a few berries about to spoil? Have your child try their hand at painting with berries! Let them use their fingers to move the berries around on paper. If your child doesn't want to touch the berry because it's too mushy, try putting it on a fork and using it as a paint-brush.

4. Head to the local craft store and have your child pick out something small to paint. Craft stores will have small wood frames or boxes. They also carry paint by numbers and terra cotta pots to paint.

**RESOURCES:**

1. *I Ain't Gonna Paint No More!* by Karen Beaumont (Harcourt Children's Books, 2005)

2. *Mouse Paint* by Ellen Stoll Walsh (Sandpiper, 1995)

3. *Sky Color* by Peter H. Reynolds (Candlewick, 2012)

# Parks

**TALK TIME:**

1. Talk to your child about the different types of parks: National, local, hiking, city, beach, dog, amusement, playground, and water parks.

2. Describe the activities that happen at a park. Talk about picnics, finding bugs, playing games, camping, barbeques, walks and hikes, animals playing, water slides, rides, food, and fun.

3. Tell your child about your favorite park or parks and describe why you enjoy them so much. If you have taken your child to a park tell them about that experience.

4. Share pictures of your adventures at a park. Take out some photos of you and describe what park you were at, who was with you, and what you did while you were there.

5. Tell your child about a park you would like to visit but have yet to have the opportunity. Do you want to see Mt. St. Helens, Disney World, or a national park that has a famous hiking trail? Describe to them why it's an important park you want to visit.

**QUESTIONS:**

1. What is the best thing to do at a park?

2. Is there something you don't like about the park?

3. Have you been to a park in the rain? Would that be fun?

4. What is your favorite park? Why?

**VOCABULARY WORDS:**

parks, national parks, water parks, beach, playground parks, city parks, local parks, hiking parks, dog parks, amusement parks, fun, excitement, enjoyment, playing, energy, tired, exhausted

**ACTIVITIES:**

1. Check out local parks and plan for at least an hour. Pack a cooler with a picnic meal, a couple of ice cream sandwiches to enjoy, or pick up some ice cream nearby to take to the park.

2. Visit a dog park. Even if you don't have a dog it's a great opportunity to see different breeds and talk about them.

3. Plan a scavenger hunt with items one might find in a park, including rocks, flowers, and signs. Create a list and allow your child to check them off or draw pictures of what they find.

4. Play a game at the park, such as hide-and-seek, or flying a kite. Roll down a hill, play on the jungle-gym, or play in the sand. Be sure to keep talking even while playing!

**RESOURCES:**

1. *A True Book: National Parks* series by David Peterson (Children's Press, 2001)

2. *The Wolves Are Back* by Jean Craighead George (Dutton Juvenile, 2008)

3. *Who Pooped in the Park?* by Gary D. Robson (Farcountry Press, 2004)

4. DVD - *Open Season movies 1, 2, and 3* (Sony Pictures, 2007)

# Road Signs

**TALK TIME:**

1. Road signs come in all different shapes and colors. Discuss how a stop sign is red and the shape of an octagon, a yellow caution sign is in the shape of a diamond, black and white signs are for one-way, and blue signs indicate information for travelers.

2. Talk about how road signs give us the location we are headed by telling us which exits to get off at, when to merge, and what is coming up head. Discuss how those help you as you drive.

3. Discuss the stoplight and the meaning behind red, yellow, and green. Discuss safety signs such as train-crossing lights and road construction signs.

4. Talk about the other safety signs of the road and explain their meanings, such as one-way, animal crossing, farm machinery crossing, road-closed, and cautionary signs for ice and rocks.

**QUESTIONS:**

1. Can you use your hand to tell someone to stop?

2. Can you Go, then Stop?

3. Can you find something red, yellow, and green in your bedroom?

4. What does red, yellow, and green mean on a stop light?

**VOCABULARY WORDS:**

road signs, yield, stop sign, green, red, yellow, stop light, road closed, railroad crossing, construction, signs, caution lights, octagon, exit signs, children at play, tractor crossing, animal crossing, car, truck, train, bus

ACTIVITIES:

1. Walk around your neighborhood with your child and have them point out stop signs, stoplights, and other road signs in the area.

2. When traveling in the car, have your child point out road signs. For the ones they are not familiar with, point them out and explain what they mean.

3. Grab some crayons, markers, and paper. Have your child create common road signs. Then have them create some of their own road signs. What color do they think road signs should be? What road signs would they make for their bedroom?

4. Utilize road signs with your child's toy cars or trains. Have the toys obey the correct road sign actions.

5. Play Red Light, Green Light with your child.

RESOURCES:

1. *Road Signs: A Hare-Y Race With a Tortoise* by Margery Cuyler (Two Lions, 2000)

2. *Signs in Our World* (DK Publishing, 2006)

# Seasons

**TALK TIME:**

1. How would you describe the word "season"? What does it mean? Explain to your child the four seasons – What is spring? Summer? Fall? Winter? What happens to your surroundings during each season? Why do we have different seasons? How long do they last? When do they change?

2. Share with your child what the seasons are like where you live. Point to things in your surroundings and explain what season you are in right now. Does it snow in the winter time? Do you have a rainy season? What are the summers like? Is there a lot of humidity in the summer or is it dry? What changes take place in your surroundings during the spring? How does the weather change during the different seasons?

3. Talk to your child about your favorite season. Do you like the winter with the cold and snow? Or do you like the spring with blossoms and green grass and leaves? What do you like about the seasons? Would you like it better if there was only one mild season all the time? Or, if you live where that is normal, would you rather live somewhere with all four seasons?

4. Tell your child about how the seasons are different around the world. For example, in the southern parts of South America, the seasons are opposite of the seasons in North America. So when it is winter in North America, it is summer in South America and visa verse. Why is that?

**QUESTIONS:**

1. What season is it right now?

2. What is the weather like in this season?

3. What is your favorite season?

4. Is there a season you don't like? What don't you like about it?

**VOCABULARY WORDS:**

summer, fall, winter, spring, weather, cold, rainy, wet, snow, white, ice, freeze, warm, melt, cool, foggy, hot, humid, dry, growth, colors, balmy, sunny, clouds, rotation, movement, climate, temperature, hemisphere, Earth, autumn, colors, wind, months, year, daylight, days, time

**ACTIVITIES:**

1. Head to your child's closet or dresser. Have them pick out what clothes they would wear in the two extreme seasons (summer and winter).

2. Grab some paper and markers. Have your child draw what symbols they think represent each of the four seasons. Then encourage your child to draw items they think go with the different seasons such as mittens for winter or a pumpkin for fall.

3. Have your child list what food they might only eat in the two extreme seasons (summer and winter). Think soup and ice cream. Now switch. Take a trip to get an ice cream cone in the middle of winter, or have some yummy soup in the summer.

4. Whatever the season is right now enjoy it with your child. Build a snowman together, plant some small flowers, go to a water park, or play in the rain and then come in for some hot apple cider.

**RESOURCES:**

1. *Here Comes Spring, and Summer and Fall and Winter* by Mary Elizabeth Murphy (DK Children, 1999)

2. *Seasons* by Blexbolex (Enchanted Lion Books, 2010)

3. *Sunshine Makes the Seasons* by Franklyn M. Branley (HarperCollins, 2005)

# Smells

## TALK TIME:

1. Share with your child some of your favorite smells. When you describe these favorite smells help your child understand the importance of the smell. Are they linked to important memories?

2. Talk to your child about smells that you do not like, whether it is food or something environmental, maybe even man-made. Discuss with your child why you do not like the smells and what might possibly make others not like the smells. Maybe they could be dangerous smells such as smells that alert us when something is wrong.

3. Explain to your child the different senses that might affect smells. You can do this by talking about sight, touch, and hearing.

4. Talk to your child about how plants, trees, and things of nature have many different smells and how man-made items may not smell at all.

## QUESTIONS:

1. What are your favorite and least favorite smells?

2. What does your parent or caregiver smell like?

3. If you close your eyes, can you smell things that you can't see?

4. What do you smell right now?

## VOCABULARY WORDS:

smells, nature smells, food smells, dangerous smells, sweet smells, sour smells, senses, nose, odor, scent, fragrance, aroma, malodor, stench, stink, reek, musky, putrid, rotten, pungent, floral, weak, strong, olfactory nerve, olfactory receptor cells

**ACTIVITIES:**

1. Put a few items in containers such as flowers, chocolate, strawberries, potato chips, or a dryer sheet. Blindfold your child and ask them to guess what the smell is. Then take turns and have your child pick some items for you to guess.

2. Now taste some of the foods and demonstrate the difference in taste when your nose is plugged vs. unplugged. Explain how smell helps increase our sense of taste.

3. Take a trip to the beach, park, or mountains, or simply go for a walk in your own backyard or neighborhood. Make stops along the way on your adventure – close your eyes and talk about what you smell.

4. Take a trip to the local nursery or home improvement store and smell the large variety of flowers.

5. Take a saucepan and add water. While the water is on low heat have your child pick out some items that might smell good. Carefully add those items to the pan. Some ideas are cinnamon, apples, orange peels, or vanilla. As the water heats up the aromas will increase in strength.

**RESOURCES:**

1. *David Smells: A Diaper David Book* by David Shannon (The Blue Sky Press, 2005)

2. *Dog Breath* by Dav Pilkey (Scholastic Paperback, 2004)

3. *Little Bunny Follows His Nose* by Katherine Howard (Golden Books, 2004)

4. *Stink and the World's Worst Super-Stinky Sneakers* (Book #3) by Megan McDonald (Candlewick, 2008)

# The Alphabet

**TALK TIME:**

1. Say the alphabet to your child from A to Z and then from Z to A. Review the vowel letters in the alphabet. Sing the alphabet song with your child and sing it often! (This is so important that it's a good idea to do this one multiple times a week.)

2. Name each letter one at a time and then make the sound that letter makes. Next talk about an animal or object that starts with each letter of the alphabet. (Example: A, aah, apple.)

3. Spell your name out for your child, and then do your child's name and any other members of the family. Spell any other favorite words you or your child have.

4. Point out a few simple items in the room. Hold the item, say it's name and then spell it. You can even do this with a body part. Take your child's foot, hold it, and spell F-O-O-T.

**QUESTIONS:**

1. Can you spell your name?

2. Can you name the vowels?

3. What letter is your favorite? Do you like upper or lowercase letters?

4. Do you like the alphabet song? Do you like spelling words?

**VOCABULARY WORDS:**

ABC's, alphabet, vowel, consonant, letter, spell, spelling, spelling-bee, sounds, names, A to Z, Z to A, words, sentences, vocabulary, reading, writing, speaking, literacy

**ACTIVITIES:**

1. Create a letter game. If your child is able, have them write each letter of the alphabet on small pieces of paper. If you need to assist, go right ahead. Then take each letter and small pieces of tape and have your child tape each letter to an item in the house, car, or in the back/front yard which the item starts with. (Example – letter T would be taped to a table.)

2. Play an alphabet scramble game using the same letters created for the game above, Have your child put the letters in order from A to Z, and for older kids from Z to A.

3. Plan a dinner or lunch, eating food that only starts with the letter A or G. Have your child pick the letter and brainstorm which foods start with the letter. Make a list with your child before you head to the grocery store, but leave time to explore more foods once you get there.

**RESOURCES:**

1. *Alphabet Under Construction* by Denise Fleming (Square Fish, 2006)

2. *Eric Carle's ABC* by Eric Carle (Grosset & Dunlap; BRDBK edition 2007)

3. *The Alphabet Book* by P.D. Eastman (Random House Books for Young Readers, 1974)

# The Country

**TALK TIME:**

1. Describe to your child what types of homes, landscapes, and livestock can be found in the country.

2. Talk to your child about living in the country. If you don't live in the country explain why. What is the difference between living in the country and living where you live?

3. Talk to your child about a time when you did something in the country. If you have never been to the country talk about what you would like to do there if you went.

4. Describe how in the country people are often far away from places like restaurants, stores, neighbors, and hospitals. Then describe activities that can be done such as camping, horseback riding, fruit picking, or cutting down a Christmas tree.

**QUESTIONS:**

1. What is your favorite thing about the country?

2. What is your least favorite thing about the country?

3. What is one thing you can only find in the country?

4. What things come from the country that you use every day?

**VOCABULARY WORDS:**

rural, country, open spaces, wildlife, animals, quiet, farms, livestock, bugs, camping, horseback riding, country style foods, petting zoo, horses, cows, sheep, chickens, grain, hay, alfalfa, feed, tractor, fields, irrigation

**ACTIVITIES:**

1. Plan a country-style dinner. Try country-style baked beans. Take your child to the grocery store and have them pick out items that one might have for dinner if they lived in the country. BBQ? Apple pie? Corn on the cob?

2. Plan a road trip to a country spot. Maybe someplace not too far from where you live. Look for local berry picking farms and even farmers markets. If something is not close by, how about a state fair that has animals which can be found in the country.

3. Play a homemade match game. Find pictures online of items found in the country and make two small printouts. Flip them over and play the match game with your child.

4. Make sun tea with your child (recipe below.)

**RECIPE: sun tea**

1. 4-6 tea bags – experiment with different flavors
2. Glass pitcher of water (amount based on tea box recommendation) with lid
3. Allow to sit in the sun for 4-5 hours
4. Place in refrigerator to cool, and add ice to glasses before drinking (Because the water never boiled the tea will only last 2-3 days.)

**RESOURCES:**

1. *Christmas in the Country* by Cynthia Rylant (Scholastic Paperback, 2005)

2. *Night in the Country* by Cynthia Rylant (Atheneum Books for Young Readers, 1991)

3. *The Way We Live in the Country* – coffee table book by Stafford Cliff (Rizzoli, 2012)

4. *When I Was Young in the Mountains* by Cynthia Rylant (Puffin 1993)

5. DVD - *Black Beauty* (Warner Home Video, 1999) and the book by the same name by Anna Sewell (Jarrold and Sons, 1877)

6. DVD - *Flicka* (20th Century, 2006) or Flicka Family Collection (20th Century, 2007)

# The Grocery Store

**TALK TIME:**

1. Explain the process of deciding what you need. Do you use a budget? Do you think about how much you will spend before going to the store? Tell your child if you make a list or not. Do you have a weekly menu?

2. Talk about the store you frequent most. Where is it located in relation to where you live? Do you drive there or walk? What is the name of the store? Why do you go to that one the most? (Is it because of the prices, products, distance, service, or something else?)

3. Share with your child what your typical trip to the store is like. Explain where you start your shopping. Do you use the deli or bakery? Tell your child what things you usually get and what parts of the store you go to.

4. And finally, talk about the check-out. Do you usually have a lot of items when you reach the cashier? Do you know any of the cashiers? What form of payment do you use? Do you ever grab that pack of gum or the candy bar that sits at the cash register as a last minute decision or just as a treat?

**QUESTIONS:**

1. What do you see when you go to the store?

2. What is your favorite thing about going to the store?

3. Why do we need a grocery store?

4. What would you do if there were no stores close by? Would you grow your own garden and raise animals like farmers do?

**VOCABULARY WORDS:**

cart, aisles, lane, product, brand, register, employee, deli, bakery, department, produce, dairy, box, can, jar, bag, price, list, ingredients, stock, shelf, kind, money, check, credit card, debit card, plastic, paper, sack, service

**ACTIVITIES:**

1. Make a list with your child of things your family needs at the grocery store. Have them help with selecting coupons and looking at the weekly ad. When you are at the store, explore an aisle you rarely go down. Point out unique and new items.

2. Play grocery store at home. Pick out a handful of non-perishable items (so there is no rush) and have your child purchase the grocery items with real or pretend money. Make sure you have bags for the groceries to go into after your child has paid.

3. Draw a store. Have your child draw their own grocery store. Have them include what items their store would carry and how much those items would cost. Also have them draw the name their store.

**RESOURCES:**

1. *At the Supermarket* by Anne Rockwell (Henry Holt and Co., 2010)

2. *Put it on the List* by Kristen Darbyshire (Dutton Juvenile, 2009)

3. *To Market, To Market* by Anne Miranda (Sandpiper, 2001)

# The Ocean

**TALK TIME:**

1. Describe the waves and the sound they make as they crash onto the shore. Talk to your child about all the oceans that cover the earth; Atlantic, Pacific, Indian, Southern and Arctic.

2. Discuss with your child why you would or would not want to live by the ocean (coast). If you currently live there, tell them why. If you have ever taken a trip out in the ocean explain your experience.

3. Talk about the ecosystem of the ocean. Discuss how the ecosystem is made of living and nonliving organisms.

4. Name some reasons why people visit to the ocean. Discuss what items they might take with them. Talk about what things you might find on the shore and in the water. If you have taken your child to the ocean, tell them how they reacted to the experience.

**QUESTIONS:**

1. What can you find in the ocean?

2. Is ocean water hot or cold?

3. Can you walk like a crab? Pucker your lips like a fish?

4. What does an ocean wave sound like?

**VOCABULARY WORDS:**

ocean, beach, coast, fish, mermaid, tuna fish, water, ocean ecosystem, Atlantic, Pacific, Indian, Southern, Arctic, ocean animals, floating ice, waves, seashells, seaweed, shore, whales, sharks, coral, salt water, saline, sail, sailboat, pilgrims, explorers, pirates

**ACTIVITIES:**

1. If you live by the ocean take your child there for a few hours. Plan to have lunch, stand in the waves, and maybe collect shells or interesting rocks.

2. If you don't live by the ocean, maybe you have a pool (any size works, even kiddy size). Plan an afternoon and pretend you are at the ocean. Have your child use their imagination and point out seagulls or crashing waves. Or maybe its wintertime and you can point out the penguins and floating chunks of ice.

3. Visit the zoo and check out the ocean-themed exhibits with your child.

4. Have fish for dinner! Have your child help. An easy one to start with is tuna fish sandwiches or fish sticks.

**RESOURCES:**

1. *Beach Day* by Karen Rossa (Clarion Books, 2001)

2. *Commotion in the Ocean* by Giles Andreae (Tiger Tales, 2002)

3. *Eye Wonder: Ocean* (DK Children, 2001)

4. DVD - *Finding Nemo* (Disney-Pixar, 2003)

5. DVD - *The Little Mermaid* (Disney, 1989)

# Trains

### TALK TIME:

1. What is a train? How would you describe it? Talk about the engine and the cars the engine pulls. Describe the tracks the train rides on. Talk about the whistle, the wheels, or the caboose. Talk about the different kinds of trains, such as coal, diesel, freight, and passenger.

2. Have you ever ridden on a train? Tell your child about your favorite train ride. Where did you go? What scenery did you pass by? What did it feel like? Who did you meet?

3. What about the history of trains? Why were they so important in the early days of travel? Talk about how trains are used for transportation of people and of vital goods we depend on every day.

4. Talk about train safety. Discuss how to look and listen for oncoming trains, as well as being safe by standing back far enough when a train approaches.

### QUESTIONS:

1. Have you ever heard a train near your house?

2. What sound do trains make?

3. Are trains big or small?

4. What do you think trains carry on them?

### VOCABULARY WORDS:

train, tracks, diesel, steam, railroad, station, engineer, whistle, locomotive, engine, conductor, tram, light rail, monorail, Orient Express, transportation, caboose, freight train, passenger train, fast, slow, ticket

**ACTIVITIES:**

1. Have your child make a train out of toys, stuffed animals, or books. Have your child push or pull the train. What happens?

2. Visit a local train station or train store. Explore the station or store. Maybe there is a local train museum that has train models set up for viewing. Does your city have a light-rail, monorail, or subway system? If so, explore those with your child. You don't need a destination to go to, just hop on for the joy of the ride.

3. Fill a train. Have your child draw a train with large windows. Have your child draw pictures in the windows of who would be on the train and what those people would bring along for the ride.

**RESOURCES:**

1. *The Blue Comet* by Rosemary Wells (Candlewich, 2010)

2. *The Goodnight Train* by June Sobel (Harcourt Children's Books, 2006)

3. *The Last Train* by Gordon M. Titcomb (Roaring Book Press, 2010)

4. *Two Little Trains* by Margaret Wise Brown (HarperCollins, 2003)

5. DVD - *The Polar Express*, both the book by Chris Van Allsburg (Houghton Mifflin, 1985) and movie (Warner Home Video, 2005)

6. DVD's - *Thomas and Friends* (Thomas the Train) by Lyons/Hit Ent.

# Exercise

**TALK TIME:**

1. Talk to your child about exercises that you like to do now and exercises you did as a child. This can be sports you played in, games that you created where you used your entire body, or work-outs. Maybe you played football, or tether ball, hopscotch, or even dodgeball. Did you like these activities? Why or why not? If you exercise now, tell your child about what types of activities you partake in to burn calories.

2. Discuss with your child why exercise is important. Describe how getting your heart rate up is beneficial as well as why it's important to stretch your muscles. You can also describe how your muscles hurt or feel sore after you exercise. Talk about the importance of rest, hydration, and how food can help relieve the soreness.

3. Talk about how animals get exercise and why it's important for their health too. You can discuss walking a dog or playing fetch. Talk about how animals can become unhealthy if they gain too much extra weight.

4. Discuss how playing a musical instrument such as the drums can be a really big arm workout. Then think of other workouts such as yoga, Tai Chi, Pilates, hiking, aerobics, lifting weights, and even how using game consoles such as Wii and Kinex can incorporate exercises.

**QUESTIONS:**

1. Do you like to exercise? Why or why not?

2. What are the benefits of exercising?

3. What are you favorite physical activities? Sports?

4. What happens to your muscles, heart and lungs when you exercise?

**VOCABULARY WORDS:**

Exercise, run, jump, spin, moving, healthy, galloping, sports, baseball, football, tennis, swimming, Frisbee, jump rope, hopscotch, slide, swing, ball, walking, biking, helmet, ski, skate, rollerblade, ice skating, soccer, bowling, kickball, football, skateboard, dancing, jumping-jacks, hiking, track and field, tai chi, aerobics, weights

**ACTIVITIES:**

1. Get out some pots and/or tupperware with a few plastic servers. Allow your child to work their arm muscles by playing the drums. Join in with your child to work your arm muscles and have fun too.

2. Sing "When the Saints Go Marching In" as you and your child march around your home.

3. Grab two small cans of soup. Ask your child to do some bicep curls. Model this by doing bicep curls yourself with cans of soup.

4. Grab a hand towel. Roll it up and place it on the floor. Ask your child to jump over it. Count aloud with your child to see how many times they can jump over it.

5. Incorporate your child into many different exercises, whether it is walking the dog and having them in a stroller, playing a game of chase in the backyard, or seeing how many jumping jacks they can do. Even try dancing!

**RESOURCES:**

1. *303 Preschooler-Approved Exercises and Activity Games* by Kimberly Wechsler (Hunter House, 2013)

2. *Fisher-Price Let's Get Moving* by Fisher-Price TM (Reader's Digest, 2010)

3. *Little Critter: Good For Me and You* by Mercer Mayer (HarperFestival, 2004)

4. *Wallie Exercises* by Steve Ettinger (Active Spud Press, 2011)

# Your Career

**TALK TIME:**

1. Describe your current job. Tell your child what you do, who you work with, and what you like and don't like about your career.

2. Talk about how you obtained the career you currently have. Tell your child what steps you took to get the job. Tell them about the interview and the skills you needed for your career.

3. If the career you currently have is not a career you want, explain what you wish to be doing instead and your plans on how you will get there.

**QUESTIONS:**

1. What career do you think is the easiest and which is the hardest?

2. What job would you never do?

3. What career do you want?

4. What careers do your friends or friends' parents have?

**VOCABULARY WORDS:**

career, job, work, paycheck, dream job, education, degree, qualifications, responsibilities, interviews, hard job, easy job, career steps, desk, chair, cubicle, office, phone, skills, company, organization, profit, non-profit, uniform, dress code, casual, business, market, sell, accounting

**ACTIVITIES:**

1. Take your child to your workplace; during work hours if allowed or after work hours if possible. If you are unable to, try taking pictures of your work, both outside and inside, to share with your child. Think of

the little things like your desk or phone.

2. Have dress up time. Allow your child to wear one of your work outfits around the house for a short time. Turn a table into their work desk with pencils, paper, and a calculator. Have them make pretend phone calls. Take photos of them at their work desk.

3. Call a small local business such as a restaurant or grocery store and ask if they would be willing to give you and your child a behind-the-scenes tour.

**RESOURCES:**

1. *Career Day* by Anne Rockwell (HarperCollins, 2000)

2. *When I Grow Up* by P.K. Hallinan (Candy Cane Press, 2006)

3. *When I Grow Up* (Little Critter) by Mercer Mayer (Random House Books for Young Readers, 2003)

4. DVD - *Bubble Guppies: On The Job* (Nickelodeon, 2013)

# What's Next? Volume 2...

Congratulations! You've just successfully completed Volume 1 in the *Child Genius 101* series. You and your child are well on your way along the path of creating a Child Genius.

Be sure to purchase the new volumes for each and every new month to keep the momentum going. Other "early childhood development" programs cost hundreds of dollars and aren't nearly as effective as simply talking with and reading to your child.

Look for Volume 2 and 3 on knowonder.com or on amazon.com. Prices start at just $4.95. Or go all digital at www.knowonder.com/register.

# Fry's Word List

The top 1,000 words in the english language

## INTRODUCTION:

What follows is a list of the top 1,000 most-commonly used words (in order of importance) in the English language. This list was compiled by Dr. Fry, hence the name, "Fry's Words."

Use these words as much as you can with your young children. A child who can understand and read just the first 300 words can read and comprehend 60% of all written materials!

Don't worry about teaching your kids to read them before they are ready. Just make sure they hear all of these words over and over and over!

## ACTIVITIES & GAMES:

If you have access to the internet, there are literally hundreds of games and activities to choose from. Go to Pinterest or Google and search for "Fry Word List Activities" or "Fry Word List Games." Here are just a couple.

1. If your child is too young to read, simply look at the Fry Words and use them in your sentences throughout the day as much as possible. Let each word trigger thoughts and ideas to talk about. Focus on just five or ten words each day. Don't feel pressure to use every single word. Just do your best to use as many as you can. Following this pattern you will go through all the Fry Words in just three months!

2. If your child is starting to read, write down 12 words on 3x5 cards. Choose 9 words your child knows and 3 words he doesn't know. Stack the cards so there are three words your child knows, then one your child does not, and continue that pattern. Have your child look through and read the cards at least once each day. As your child learns new words, congratulate him and add a new word he doesn't know to the stack.

## First 100

the
of
and
a
to
in
is
you
that
it

he
was
for
on
are
as
with
his
they
I

at
be
this
have
from
or
one
had
by
words

but
not
what
all
were
we
when
your
can
said

there
use
an
each
which
she
do
how
their
if

will
up
other
about
out
many
then
them
these
so

some
her
would
make
like
him
into
time
has
look

two
more
write
go
see
number
no
way
could
people

my
than
first
water
been
called
who
oil
sit
now

find
long
down
day
did
get
come
made
may
part

## Second 100

over
new
sound
take
only
little
work
know
place
years

live
me
back
give
most
very
after
things
our
just

name
good
sentence
man
think
say
great
where
help
through

much
before
line
right
too
means
old
any
same
tell

boy
follow
came
want
show
also
around
form
three
small

set
put
end
does
another
well
large
must
big
even

such
because
turn
here
why
ask
went
men
read
need

land
different
home
us
move
try
kind
hand
picture
again

change
off
play
spell
air
away
animal
house
point
page

letter
mother
answer
found
study
still
learn
should
America
world

## Third 100

| | | | |
|---|---|---|---|
| high | along | sea | cut |
| every | might | began | young |
| near | close | grow | talk |
| add | something | took | soon |
| food | seem | river | list |
| between | next | four | song |
| own | hard | carry | being |
| below | open | state | leave |
| country | example | once | family |
| plant | begin | book | it's |
| | | | |
| last | life | hear | |
| school | always | stop | |
| father | those | without | |
| keep | both | second | |
| tree | paper | late | |
| never | together | miss | |
| start | got | idea | |
| city | group | enough | |
| earth | often | eat | |
| eyes | run | face | |
| | | | |
| light | important | watch | |
| thought | until | far | |
| head | children | Indian | |
| under | side | real | |
| story | feet | almost | |
| saw | car | let | |
| left | mile | above | |
| don't | night | girl | |
| few | walk | sometimes | |
| while | white | mountains | |

## Fourth 100

body
music
color
stand
sun
questions
fish
area
mark
dog

top
ship
across
today
during
short
better
best
however
low

five
step
morning
passed
vowel
true
hundred
against
pattern
numeral

town
I'll
unit
figure
certain
field
travel
wood
fire
upon

horse
birds
problem
complete
room
knew
since
ever
piece
told

hours
black
products
happened
whole
measure
remember
early
waves
reached

table
north
slowly
money
map
farm
pulled
draw
voice
seen

usually
didn't
friends
easy
heard
order
red
door
sure
become

listen
wind
rock
space
covered
fast
several
hold
himself
toward

cold
cried
plan
notice
south
sing
war
ground
fall
king

**Fifth 100**

done
English
road
half
ten
fly
gave
box
finally
wait

correct
oh
quickly
person
became
shown
minutes
strong
verb
stars

front
feel
fact
inches
street
decided
contain
course
surface
produce

building
ocean
class
note
nothing
rest
carefully
scientists
inside
wheels

stay
green
known
island
week
less
machine
base
ago
stood

plane
system
behind
ran
round
boat
game
force
brought
understand

warm
common
bring
explain
dry
though
language
shape
deep
thousands

yes
clear
equation
yet
government
filled
heat
full
hot
check

object
am
rule
among
noun
power
cannot
able
six
size

dark
ball
material
special
heavy
fine
pair
circle
include
built

## Sixth 100

can't
matter
square
syllables
perhaps
bill
felt
suddenly
test
direction

center
farmers
ready
anything
divided
general
energy
subject
Europe
moon

region
return
believe
dance
members
picked
simple
cells
paint
mind

love
cause
rain
exercise
eggs
train
blue
wish
drop
developed

window
difference
distance
heart
site
sum
summer
wall
forest
probably

legs
sat
main
winter
wide
written
length
reason
kept
interest

arms
brother
race
present
beautiful
store
job
edge
past
sign

record
finished
discovered
wild
happy
beside
gone
sky
grass
million

west
lay
weather
root
instruments
meet
third
months
paragraph
raised

represent
soft
whether
clothes
flowers
shall
teacher
held
describe
drive

**Seventh 100**

cross
speak
solve
appear
metal
son
either
ice
sleep
village

copy
free
hope
spring
case
laughed
nation
quite
type
themselves

possible
gold
milk
quiet
natural
lot
stone
act
build
middle

surprise
French
died
beat
exactly
remain
dress
cat
couldn't
fingers

factors
result
jumped
snow
ride
care
floor
hill
pushed
baby

temperature
bright
lead
everyone
method
section
lake
iron
within
dictionary

speed
count
consonant
someone
sail
rolled
bear
wonder
smiled
angle

buy
century
outside
everything
tall
already
instead
phrase
soil
bed

hair
age
amount
scale
pounds
although
per
broken
moment
tiny

fraction
Africa
killed
melody
bottom
trip
hole
poor
let's
fight

**Eight 100**

row
least
catch
climbed
wrote
shouted
continued
itself
else
plains

gas
England
burning
design
joined
foot
law
ears
glass
you're

grew
skin
valley
cents
key
president
brown
trouble
cool
cloud

lost
sent
symbols
wear
bad
save
experiment
engine
alone
drawing

east
choose
single
touch
information
express
mouth
yard
equal
decimal

yourself
control
practice
report
straight
rise
statement
stick
party
seeds

suppose
woman
coast
bank
period
wire
pay
clean
visit
bit

whose
received
garden
please
strange
caught
fell
team
God
captain

direct
ring
serve
child
desert
increase
history
cost
maybe
business

separate
break
uncle
hunting
flow
lady
students
human
art
feeling

**Ninth 100**

supply
corner
electric
insects
crops
tone
hit
sand
doctor
provide

thus
won't
cook
bones
mall
board
modern
compound
mine
wasn't

fit
addition
belong
safe
soldiers
guess
silent
trade
rather
compare

crowd
poem
enjoy
elements
indicate
except
expect
flat
seven
interesting

sense
string
blow
famous
value
wings
movement
pole
exciting
branches

thick
blood
lie
spot
bell
fun
loud
consider
suggested
thin

position
entered
fruit
tied
rich
dollars
send
sight
chief
Japanese

stream
planets
rhythm
eight
science
major
observe
tube
necessary
weight

meat
lifted
process
army
hat
property
particular
swim
terms
current

park
sell
shoulder
industry
wash
block
spread
cattle
wife
sharp

## Tenth 100

| | | | |
|---|---|---|---|
| company | opposite | workers | cows |
| radio | wrong | Washington | track |
| we'll | chart | Greek | arrived |
| action | prepared | women | located |
| capital | pretty | bought | sir |
| factories | solution | led | seat |
| settled | fresh | march | division |
| yellow | shop | northern | effect |
| isn't | suffix | create | underline |
| southern | especially | British | view |
| truck | shoes | difficult | |
| fair | actually | match | |
| printed | nose | win | |
| wouldn't | afraid | doesn't | |
| ahead | dead | steel | |
| chance | sugar | total | |
| born | adjective | deal | |
| level | fig | determine | |
| triangle | office | evening | |
| molecules | huge | hoe | |
| France | gun | rope | |
| repeated | similar | cotton | |
| column | death | apple | |
| western | score | details | |
| church | forward | entire | |
| sister | stretched | corn | |
| oxygen | experience | substances | |
| plural | rose | smell | |
| various | allow | tools | |
| agreed | fear | conditions | |

# Register:

Register on our website (www.knowonder.com/register) to get **FREE** access to over 500 original stories, education tools and other resources to help you give the gift of literacy to your child, each and every day.

# About knowonder!

Knowonder is a leading publisher of engaging, daily content that drives literacy; the most important factor in a child's success.

Parents and educators use Knowonder tools and content to promote reading, creativity, and thinking skills in children from zero to twelve.

Knowonder's Literacy Program - delivered through storybook collections and other meaningful material - delivers original, compelling content and new stories every day, creating an opportunity for parents to connect to their children in ways that significantly improve their children's success.

Ultimately, Knowonder's mission is to eradicate illiteracy and improve education success through content that is affordable, accessible, and effective.

Learn more at

**www.knowonder.com**

# About the Author:

Phillip J. Chipping is a born entrepreneur, a natural storyteller and the creative force behind knowonder! Phillip learned his deep love of reading from an early age, which in turn nurtured his own imagination and creativity. This fostered in him a desire to find innovative solutions for everyday problems.

Born and raised in Salt Lake City, Utah, Phillip had the inspiration for knowonder! while living with his family in England as the Managing Director of ZAGG Ltd., the UK arm of ZAGG Inc.; a company Phillip founded. He saw his children's love of reading blossom when they had a new story each day and decided to bring that concept home when they returned. Phillip now lives with his wife and four children in Cache Valley, Utah.

Phillip is now pursuing a degree in Early Childhood Development. His personal passion for literacy has driven him to study and research the topic deeply and apply his findings to real-world situations and families in profound and meaningful ways.

# About the Author:

Savannah Hendricks holds a degree in Early Childhood Education. She worked as a nanny for seven years, as well as with special needs preschoolers. She discovered through her work that children learn the best when you take the time to be a part of their world. She currently works with developmentally disabled teenagers. Her main focus is to bring the enjoyment of reading to children and to help others understand the importance of early childhood education through spending quality time with children.

Savannah also loves to write! Her stories have been included in numerous magazines such as knowonder!, Highlights High Five, Stories for Children Magazine, Hollins, and Reunions.

# Notes:

1. Dr. Betty Hart and Dr. Todd Risley, *Meaningful Differences in the Everyday Lives of American Children* (Baltimore, MD: Brookes, Publishing, 1996)

2. Dr. Betty Hart and Dr. Todd Risley, *Meaningful Differences in the Everyday Lives of American Children* (Baltimore, MD: Brookes, Publishing, 1996)

3. Clayton M. Christensen, *Disrupting Class: How Disruptive Innovation Will Change the Way the World Learns* (McGraw Hill, 2008)

4. Jim Trelease, *The Read-Aloud Handbook* (The Penguin Group, sixth-edition, 2006, p. 13)

5. Jim Trelease, *The Read-Aloud Handbook* (The Penguin Group, sixth-edition, 2006, p. 16)

6. Dr. Betty Hart and Dr. Todd Risley, *Meaningful Differences in the Everyday Lives of American Children* (Baltimore, MD: Brookes, Publishing, 1996)

7. Dr. Betty Hart and Dr. Todd Risley, *Meaningful Differences in the Everyday Lives of American Children* (Baltimore, MD: Brookes, Publishing, 1996)

8. Jim Trelease, *The Read-Aloud Handbook* (The Penguin Group, sixth-edition, 2006)

9. Dr. Betty Hart and Dr. Todd Risley, *Meaningful Differences in the Everyday Lives of American Children* (Baltimore, MD: Brookes, Publishing, 1996)

# Download:

"By age three, children from privileged families have heard 30 million more words than children from poor families. By kindergarten the gap is even greater. **The consequences are catastrophic.**" – American Educator, Spring 2003

A **free six-page summary** of the findings from the *Meaningful Differences* research project can be downloaded for parents from the link below. This is a summary written by the researchers, Drs. Hart and Risley.

http://www.knowonder.com/The-Early-Catastrophe

Made in the USA
Lexington, KY
28 January 2015